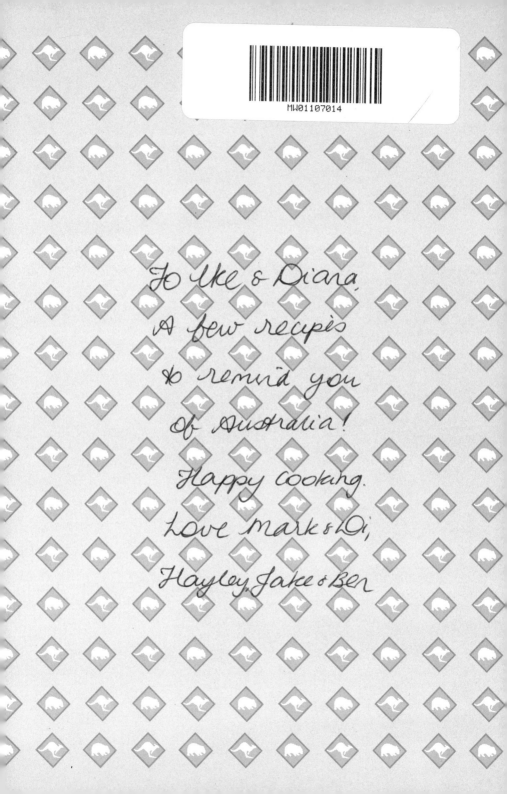

To Uke & Diana,

A few recipes

to remind you

of Australia!

Happy cooking.

Love Mark & Di,

Hayley, Jake & Ben

GREAT
Australian
RECIPES

First published in 1993 by
South Land Design Pty. Ltd.
P.O. Box 467, Forestville, NSW 2087, Sydney, Australia.

© South Land Design Pty. Ltd
Editor & Designer Joe Reynolds
Text © Diana Dasey
Illustrations Cynthia Morissey

Printed in Australia

ISBN 1 875752 00 5

Australia's traditional cuisine and its short but colourful history are firmly intertwined. From the most unlikely of backgrounds a distinct and imaginative way of cooking has evolved.

The country's first European settlers were British convicts and their keepers in 1788 - many of whom came from large, crowded towns and knew little about cooking or growing food.

In the early days of the settlement most were homesick for the comforting cooking of their mother England, and many nearly starved despite the abundance of naturally occurring food.

Native Aborigines had survived for thousands of years on a rich diet of yams, fish, turtles, lizards, wild fruits and nuts - all of which the first settlers found unpalatable or simply disgusting. But while their eyes were closed to the natural bounty of foods around them, these first European settlers weren't totally lacking in imagination.

Through ingenuity - and necessity - variations on traditional English recipes evolved with a distinctly Australian flavour. Local climatic conditions and food shortages gave rise to an original style of cooking which filled the bellies of generations of farmers, miners and everyday Australians.

Since the Second World War immigration from around the world has seen Australia become very much a multi cultural country. In step with the changing face of its people, Australian cooking has evolved too and Australians now enjoy a truly international cuisine. Influences from every European country and all parts of Asia have put an end to the days of "meat and three veg" - once our staple diet.

Even Australia's naturally occurring foods - bush tucker - which the first settlers so quickly rejected, are coming into vogue. But while eating habits have changed, there is still a great affection for the comfortable, familiar recipes of the past. This book is dedicated to the early British settlers - and the style of cooking they pioneered.

FISH MORNAY

Most Australian households had their own version of this dish. Some women used fresh cooked fish instead of the canned. Others used more eggs and no fish at all and others daringly used cans of creamed soups instead of making a white sauce.

Serves 4

4 level tablespoons butter
4 level tablespoons plain (all purpose) flour
2 cups milk
250g (8oz) canned pink salmon, drained and with bones removed
squeeze lemon juice
4 hard cooked eggs, peeled and cut into quarters
pinch of cayenne pepper
2 tablespoons grated Cheddar cheese
dried breadcrumbs

Melt the butter in a saucepan and stir in the flour. Cook for one minute over a low heat. Add the milk gradually and cook until the sauce thickens, stirring all the time. Mix in the the fish, lemon juice, eggs, cayenne pepper and the cheese. Spoon into a greased ovenproof dish and sprinkle on the breadcrumbs. Bake in a moderate oven for 15 minutes or until browned.

KANGAROO TAIL SOUP

Recipes for Kangaroo Tail Soup need the instruction : First catch your Kangaroo - as Kangaroo meat is not usually sold commercially for human consumption. The soup tastes a little like Ox Tail Soup but Kangaroo flesh is much stronger and more gamey.

Serves 8

2 tablespoons oil
1 kangaroo tail, skinned and cut into joints
1 large onion, chopped
1 medium carrot, peeled and chopped
2 stalks celery, chopped
10 cups water
1 bay leaf
12 peppercorns
4 stalks parsley
1/2 teaspoon dried thyme
1/2 teaspoon dried rosemary
2 large onions, extra, sliced
2 medium carrots, extra, sliced
2 stalks celery, extra, sliced
1/2 cup barley
1 teaspoon tomato paste
1/3 cup dry sherry
chopped parsley

Heat the oil in a large saucepan and brown the kangaroo joints, a few at a time. Lift out and drain. Fry the chopped onion, carrot and celery until brown. Drain away all the fat and return the browned kangaroo joints to the saucepan with the water, bayleaf, peppercorns and herbs. Bring to the boil and skim away any scum. Cover with a lid and cook slowly over a low heat for 4 hours. Lift out the meat and strain the stock. Cool and refrigerate overnight. Remove the fat from the top of the soup and pull the meat from the kangaroo joints.

Cook stock, kangaroo meat, extra onion, carrots, celery, barley and tomato paste for 30 minutes or until the vegetables are cooked. Add sherry and chopped parsley just before serving.

PASSIONFRUIT FLUMMERY

There are many, many ways of making this old fashioned fruit dessert. The Scots once thickened it with oatmeal, the Dutch used isinglass and egg yolks while Spanish cooks like rice flour. Australians prefer a mix of flour and gelatine and make it distinctively their own by using fresh passionfruit.

Serves 4

3 level teaspoons unflavoured gelatine
1/2 cup sugar
2 level tablespoons plain flour
1 cup water
1 cup orange juice
1/3 cup passionfruit pulp

Blend together the gelatine, sugar, flour and water and place in a small saucepan. Bring to the boil over a moderate heat and cook until the mixture thickens, stirring all the time. Pour into a large mixing bowl and allow to cool. Mix in the orange juice and passionfruit pulp. Chill until the mixture begins to set around the edges and beat with an electric mixer for five minutes or until the mixture is thick and foamy. Chill and serve with custard or cream.

CARPETBAG STEAK

Any cut of thick tender expensive beef steak can be used to make this uniquely Australian dish. Poor people have even been known to cut and fill thick sausages with the oysters.

Serves 1

250g (8oz) tender steak, 4cm (2 inches) thick
salt and black pepper
squeeze of lemon juice
6 fresh oysters
1 tablespoon of butter
2 teaspoons oil

Cut a deep pocket in the steak and season with the salt and pepper. Squeeze the lemon juice over the oysters and pack into the pocket. Seal the pocket with a skewer. Heat the butter and oil in a heavy frying pan over a moderately high heat. Add the steak and cook 3 to 4 minutes per side for very rare and 5 to 6 minutes for medium rare. Serve immediately with a sauteed potatoes and a green salad.

FISH CAKES

Australians first take away-food was fish and chips from the local fish shop on Friday nights. On no-money Fridays they ate fish cakes like these at home.

Serves 4

2 tablespoons butter
1 medium sized onion, finely chopped
2 teaspoons finely chopped parsley
2 cups cold mashed potato
250g (8oz) cooked and flaked boneless fish, fresh or canned
1/2 level teaspoon salt
1/4 level teaspoon cayenne pepper
1 teaspoon lemon juice
1 egg, beaten
dried breadcrumbs
oil or butter for shallow frying

Mix together butter, onion, parsley, potato, fish, salt, pepper and lemon juice. Shape into flat cakes and dip in the beaten egg and then the breadcrumbs. Heat the oil and cook for 3 minutes on each side. Drain on kitchen paper and serve with tartare sauce.

Tartare sauce.

1 cup mayonnaise
3 spring onions, finely chopped
1 tablespoon capers
1 small gherkin, finely chopped
1 tablespoon French mustard

Mix together all ingredients and let stand for 30 minutes before using.

SAGO PLUM PUDDING

This pudding is for all of those women who didn't manage to make a super Christmas pudding weeks or months or even a year before Christmas. It is not as complicated to make as a traditional pudding, and it goes well with Brandy Custard.

Serves 4 to 6
4 level tablespoons sago
1 cup milk
60g (2 oz) butter
1/2 cup sugar
1 level teaspoon bicarbonate of soda (baking soda)
1 cup fresh white breadcrumbs
1/4 cup plain (all purpose) flour
pinch of salt
1/2 cup sultanas (golden raisins)
1/2 cup seedless raisins
1/2 cup chopped dates

Soak the sago in milk overnight. Grease a medium sized pudding basin with butter and cut a piece of baking parchment to line the bottom. Beat the butter and sugar together and mix in the soaked sago and the remaining ingredients. Place in the greased basin. Cover the pudding with a double thickness of lightly greased greaseproof paper and clip on the lid. Stand the basin in a saucepan of rapidly boiling water so that the basin is half submerged and steam for 21/2 to 3 hours. Serve hot with Brandy Custard.

Brandy Custard
2 eggs
2 level tablespoons sugar
2 cups milk
2 tablespoons brandy

Beat together the eggs and the sugar. Warm the milk in a saucepan until nearly boiling and pour onto the beaten eggs. Place the mixture in the top half of a double boiler over simmering water and cook until the custard coats the back of a spoon, stirring all the time. Do not let the custard overheat or it will curdle. Add the brandy and serve warm.

AUSTRALIAN MEAT PIE

All true blue Australians have eaten meat pie at some time in their lives and all soon learn the best way to eat a meat pie without getting any drops of gravy on their clothes. A traditional meat pie once was just plain beef, but vegetables, curry and different meats are now being put into pies.

Serves 6

500g (1lb 2oz) stewing steak cut into small cubes
1/2 cup plain (all purpose) flour
2 tablespoons oil
1 onion, finely chopped
2 beef stock cubes
1 1/2 cups of water
black pepper
1 1/2 level teaspoon ground nutmeg
1 tablespoon Worcestershire sauce
2 tablespoons chopped parsley
200g (7oz) short crust pastry sheets for bases of pies
200g (7oz) puff pastry sheets for tops of pies

Roll the meat cubes in flour. Heat the oil and brown the meat and onions. Add the beef stock cubes, pepper, water, nutmeg, Worcestershire sauce and the parsley and cover with a lid. Cook over a low heat for one hour, stirring every now and then, until the meat is cooked. Cool completely. Line six small pie pans with the short crust pastry and three quarters fill with the cooled filling. Moisten the cut edges of the bottom pastry with water and cut the puff pastry tops. Press lightly to seal the edges and brush lightly with milk and pierce the centres with a sharp knife to allow steam to escape. Bake in a hot oven for 20 to 25 minutes or until the pastry is crisp and golden brown.

PUMPKIN SCONES

Queenslanders believe that their Queensland blue pumpkin is one of the best flavoured pumpkins in the world and serve it boiled or baked as a vegetable and use it to make sweet scones, or as Americans call them, biscuits.

Makes 8

2 cups plain (all purpose) flour
3 level teaspoons baking powder
pinch of salt
30g (1oz.) butter
1/4 cup castor (superfine) sugar
1 cup steamed pumpkin, drained and mashed
1 egg, lightly beaten
extra milk for glazing

Sift the flour, baking powder and salt into a bowl and rub in the butter with fingertips. Add the sugar, pumpkin and egg and mix quickly into a soft dough. Knead very gently on a lightly floured board and pat the dough to 2.5cm (1 inch) thickness. Cut into rounds with a sharp cutter and place in a well greased 20cm (8 inch) pan. Brush the tops with extra milk. Bake in a very hot oven for 15 to 20 minutes or until cooked. For a soft crusted scone, wrap the hot scones in a clean cloth for a few minutes before serving.

BUBBLE AND SQUEAK

Most Australian children liked the name of this dish better than they liked the taste of it. It needed a great deal of imagination to see the bubble and hear the squeak as it cooked. For mothers, it was a great way to use up leftovers.

Serves 2 to 4

3 tablespoons butter or beef dripping
1 medium onion, chopped
1/4 medium cabbage, shredded and cooked
salt and pepper
1 cup cold mashed potato
1 cup cold mashed pumpkin

Heat the butter in a large frying pan and cook the onion until soft and golden, stirring every now and then. Add the cabbage and cook for one minute, stirring all the time. Season with salt and pepper. Mix in the potato and pumpkin and press down flat. Cook over a moderate heat until the underside is lightly browned. Turn and cook the other side.

LEMON DELICIOUS PUDDING

In the past many Australians suburban backyards had a lemon tree growing in the fowl yard so there was always a good supply of lemons and eggs to make this simple family pudding.

Serves 4

2 level tablespoons plain (all purpose) flour
1/2 level teaspoon baking powder
pinch of salt
2 level tablespoons soft butter
2/3 cup castor (superfine) sugar
1/4 cup lemon juice
2 teaspoons finely grated lemon rind
2 egg yolks, lightly beaten
I cup milk
2 egg whites, beaten until stiff

Sift the flour, baking powder and salt together. Beat the butter and sugar until light and fluffy. Sprinkle the sifted dry ingredients over the butter and sugar and fold in the lemon juice and grated rind. Mix together the egg yolks and milk and add to the mixture. Gently fold in the beaten egg whites. Pour into a greased ovenproof dish and stand the dish in a pan of cold water. Bake in a moderate oven for 40 minutes or until cooked.

ROAST LEG OF LAMB
WITH VEGETABLES, GRAVY AND MINT SAUCE

Meat was once very cheap in Australia and newcomers to the country were often amused or appalled at how many Australians could eat meat three times a day, at breakfast, lunch and dinner. In these health conscious times much less meat is eaten but there is always going to be a place on Australian dinner tables for an old fashioned roast dinner.

Serves 4 to 6
2kg (4lb) leg of lamb
salt and black pepper
500g (16oz) old potatoes, peeled and cut into quarters
300g (10oz) pumpkin, peeled and cut into quarters
300g (10oz) sweet potato,peeled and cut into large rounds
4 to 6 large onions, peeled
2 level tablespoons plain (all purpose) flour
2 cups hot water

Sprinkle the meat with salt and pepper and place fat side up on a rack in a large deep sided baking dish. Roast in a hot oven for 11/2 to 2 hours. Put the potatoes in a saucepan of cold water and bring to a boil. Cook for 5 minutes and then drain and dry and place to the side of the roasting meat with the rest of the vegetables for the last hour of cooking. Spoon hot fat over the vegetables, once or twice. Lift out the meat and let stand in a warm place for 10 to 15 minutes before carving. When the vegetables are cooked remove from pan and keep warm on a heated serving platter while making the gravy. Drain away all but 2 tablespoons of fat from the baking dish and heat the dish over a medium heat. Add the flour and cook for two minutes, stirring all the time. Pour in the hot water, stirring all the time. Cook for 3 minutes until thickened. Strain into a gravy boat and add extra salt and pepper if necessary.

Mint sauce.
1/2 cup mint leaves,chopped
1 tablespoon boiling water
sugar
1 tablespoon
2 tablespoons white vinegar

Place the chopped mint in a small bowl and pour on the boiling water. Add the remaining ingredients and serve warm.

GOLDEN SYRUP STEAMED PUDDING

Australians warmed themselves and their houses up on cold winter nights with steamed puddings that took hours to cook in large saucepan of boiling water. These days a microwave oven can nearly duplicate the perfection of a steamed pudding, but not completely.

Serves 6

1 1/2 cups plain (all purpose) flour
3 level teaspoons baking powder
3 level tablespoons golden syrup (light treacle) or honey
125g (4oz) butter
1/2 cup castor (superfine) sugar
few drops vanilla essence
2 eggs
1/2 cup milk

Sift the flour and the baking powder together. Grease a small pudding basin with butter and line the base with a round of baking parchment. Spoon the golden syrup onto the baking parchment. Beat the butter, sugar and vanilla essence together until light and fluffy and add the eggs one at a time. Fold in the sifted flour alternately with the milk and spoon the mixture on to the golden syrup in the basin. Cover the basin with two sheets of greased paper or aluminium foil and tie tightly with a string. Lower the pudding into a saucepan of boiling water with the water coming half way up the sides of the basin. Cover and cook slowly for 1 1/2 hours. Let stand for 5 minutes before turning out of the basin. Serve hot with Sweet White Sauce.

Sweet White Sauce

1 1/2 level tablespoons cornflour (cornstarch)
1 cup milk
1 level tablespoon sugar
vanilla essence

Blend the cornflour with a little milk. Place the remainder of the milk in a saucepan with the sugar and bring to the boil. When nearly boiling remove from the heat and add the blended cornflour and milk. Return to the heat and cook for three minutes, stirring all the time. Add the vanilla and serve warm.

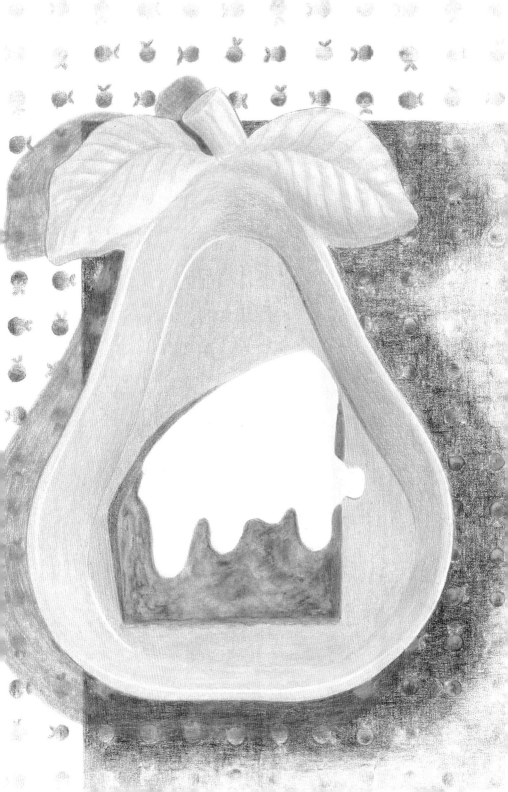

GOLDEN SYRUP CARAMEL SAUCE

Australian children have been spooning this simple superb sauce over their ice cream for years and years and years.

I level tablespoon butter
4 level tablespoons brown sugar
I tablespoon golden syrup (light treacle)
2 tablespoons sweetened condensed milk
4 tablespoons hot water

Melt the butter in a heavy saucepan and add the brown sugar, golden syrup and condensed milk. Cook over a moderate heat until the mixture turns a rich caramel colour and leaves the sides of the saucepan, stirring all the time. Remove from the heat and mix in the hot water a little at a time. Return to the heat and cook for another 2 minutes. Serve hot or cold.

CHRISTMAS CAKE

Australian women make their Christmas cakes weeks and weeks
before the 25th of December so that the flavours of all the ingredients
blend beautifully together as the cakes mature.

1/2 cup dried apricots, chopped
13/4 cup dates, stoned and chopped
21/2 cups sultanas (golden raisins)
21/2 cups seedless raisins
3/4 cup glace (candied) cherries, chopped
3/4 cup dark rum
250g (8oz) butter
11/2 cups light brown sugar
5 large eggs
1 tablespoon glycerine (optional)
1 teaspoon vanilla essence
1 teaspoon almond essence
1 tablespoon golden syrup (light treacle)
1 tablespoon plum jam
finely grated rind and juice of 1 lemon
2 cups plain (all purpose) flour
1 level teaspoon salt
1 level teaspoon cinnamon
1 level teaspoon nutmeg
1/2 level teaspoon ground ginger
1/2 level teaspoon ground cloves
1 cup almond slivers
11/2 cups blanched almonds for decoration
2 tablespoons extra rum

Place all the fruit and the rum in a large bowl. Cover and leave to stand for
at least 8 hours. Line a 20 cm (8 inch) square or round cake pan with 2 layers
of baking parchment. Cream the butter and sugar until light and fluffy and
add the eggs one at a time beating well after each one is added. Add the
essences, golden syrup, jam, lemon rind and juice. Sift the flour and salt and
spices together and add alternately to the creamed mixture with the soaked
fruit and almond slivers. Place in the lined pan and press the blanched
almonds into the top of the cake. Bake in a slow oven for 3 to 31/2 hours or
until a skewer inserted in the centre of the cake comes out dry. If the cake is
browning too much, cover loosely with aluminium foil. Pour on the extra rum
and wrap the cake still in the pan in a large towel so that it cools slowly.
Leave until completely cold before removing.

ANZACS

The Australian and New Zealand Army Corp was a unit of Australian and New Zealanders who fought together in the First World War. Their womenfolk made long lasting and sturdy biscuits and sent them with other loving comforts of home such as knitted socks.

Makes 40

1 cup rolled oats
1 cup desiccated (flaked coconut)
1 cup plain (all purpose) flour
1 cup sugar
125g(4oz) butter or margarine
1 level tablespoon golden syrup (light treacle)
1 level teaspoon bicarbonate of soda (baking soda)
2 tablespoons boiling water

Place the rolled oats, coconut, flour and sugar in a mixing bowl. Heat the butter and golden syrup in a saucepan over a low heat. Mix the bicarbonate of soda and boiling water together and add to the saucepan. Combine all the ingredients to make a moist but firm mixture. Place on greased baking trays, allowing for 5cm (2 1/2 inches) for spreading. Bake in a moderately slow oven for 20 minutes or until golden brown and cooked. Cool on baking trays for 5 minutes to firm up before removing to a wire rack to cool. Store in airtight containers when completely cold.

DAMPER

Australian drovers and bushmen baked this simple bread in camp ovens buried deep in the hot ashes of an outback camp fires. City folks bake it in a hot oven or shape it into small rolls, wrapped in several layers of aluminium foil to cook on the barbie, i.e. the barbecue.

Serves 4

4 cups plain (all purpose) flour
6 level teaspoons baking powder
1 level teaspoon salt
3/4 cup milk
3/4 cup water
extra flour
extra milk

Sift the flour, baking powder and salt into a bowl and make a well in the centre. Pour in the milk and water all at once and using a table knife, very quickly mix ingredients, using a cutting action.

To cook in a camp oven, use a double quantity of ingredients. Knead the dough very lightly with the extra flour and shape into a round. Place in a well greased camp oven, cut a deep cross in the top. Brush the surface with the extra milk and dust with flour. Cover with the lid and bake in the hot ashes of a camp fire for about 30 to 45 minutes or until cooked. Eat while still warm with butter and golden syrup (light treacle).

To cook in an oven, shape the dough into a round and cut a deep cross in the top. Brush the top with milk and dust with the extra flour. Bake in a hot oven for 45 minutes or until cooked and golden brown.

TOFFEE

Australian children pester their mothers to make toffee or, better still, to be allowed to make it for themselves. Toffees like these are always on sale at Spring Fetes and any other money raising affairs run mainly by mothers.

Makes 12

3 cups sugar
1 cup cold water
1/4 cup white vinegar
hundreds and thousands (nonpareils)

Place 12 paper patty cases on a tray. Put the sugar, water and vinegar in a heavy saucepan and stir over a low heat until the sugar is dissolved. Without stirring bring to a rapid boil over a high heat and boil for 12 to 14 minutes or until the mixture is dissolved. Without stirring bring to a rapid boil over a high heat and boil for 12 to 14 minutes or until the mixture reaches the "hard crack" stage (see below). Remove from the heat and stand for two minutes or until the bubbles disappear. Pour into the paper patty cases and sprinkle with the hundreds and thousands. Leave for 1 hour.

To test for the "hard crack" stage, drop a little toffee in cold water. If the toffee hardens, it has cooked.

COLONIAL GOOSE

The "goose" in this something-of-a-joke recipe isn't really a goose at all but is a boned stuffed leg of lamb. Some cooks like to carry the fun further by stuffing a partially boned forequarter of lamb and arranging the shank to look like the head and neck of a goose.

Serves 4 to 6
1 boned leg of lamb, about 2kg (4lb)
Stuffing
30g (1oz) butter, melted
1 medium sized onion, finely chopped
2 cups fresh white breadcrumbs
1/2 level teaspoon black pepper
1/2 level teaspoon of salt
1 level teaspoon mixed herbs (oregano, thyme, basil, rosemary)
1 egg, beaten
Marinade
2 small carrots, roughly chopped
2 medium sized onions, chopped
1 bay leaf
3 stalks parsley
1 stalk celery, chopped
1 cup dry red wine
1 tablespoon black peppercorns
Sauce
1 cup chicken stock
2 level teaspoons arrowroot mixed with a little cold water

Mix together all the stuffing ingredients and pack into the boned leg of lamb. Sew up or tie the meat to make a neat shape and place in a stainless steel or glass bowl. Mix together the marinade ingredients and pour over the meat. Cover the meat and refrigerate for at least 8 hours. Turn the meat in the marinade every now and then. Lift out the meat from the marinade and keep 1/4 cup of the marinade. Place the meat on a rack in a roasting pan and roast in a moderate oven for 1 1/2 to 2 hours or until cooked. Remove the meat to a platter, and keep warm, remove string if used. Let stand for at least 15 minutes before carving. Drain fat from the roasting pan and heat the pan over a medium heat. Add the 1/4 cup of the reserved marinade and the chicken stock. Bring to the boil and thicken with the dissolved arrowroot. Strain the sauce into a gravy boat and serve with the cooked meat.

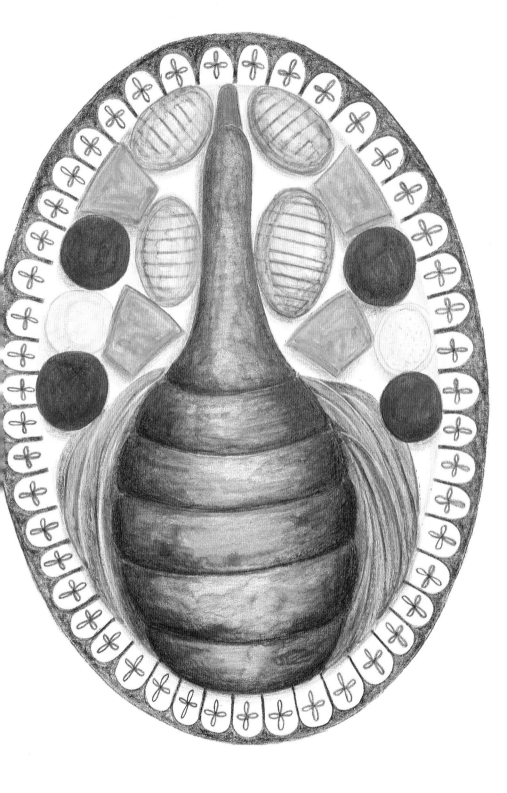

GRAMMA TART

Gramma Tarts are kissing cousins to the American Pumpkin Pie, but gramma pumpkins have a different taste and texture to regular pumpkin.

Serves 6 to 8

500g (16oz) steamed hot gramma pumpkin, drained and mashed
2 level teaspoons butter
1 egg, lightly beaten
1/2 cup light brown sugar
1 teaspoon finely grated lemon rind
2 tablespoons lemon juice
1/2 level teaspoon cinnamon
1/4 level teaspoon ground nutmeg
1/4 level teaspoon ground cloves
1/4 cup sultanas (golden raisins)
23cm (9 inch) unbaked short crust pastry pie shell
milk for glazing
icing (confectioner's) sugar

Mix together gramma, butter, egg, sugar, lemon rind, juice, spices and sultanas and pour into pastry shell. Smooth the top and decorate with scraps of pastry. Brush with milk. Bake in a moderately hot oven for 10 minutes, reduce heat to moderate and cook for a further 10 to 15 minutes. Sprinkle with icing sugar while warm and serve with custard or whipped cream.

LAMB'S FRY AND BACON

Once Australians used to sit down every morning to a hearty hot cooked breakfast of porridge, a meat dish of some kind, toast and tea. Now, breakfasts are more likely to be a glass of fruit juice, a plate of cereal with milk, a slice or two of wholegrain toasted bread and a cup of coffee. But some of the best loved breakfast dishes have moved into dinner time and this lamb's liver dish is one of them.

Serves 2

4 lean bacon rashers, with the rind removed
2 level tablespoons plain (all purpose) flour
salt and pepper for seasoning
1 lamb's liver, trimmed and cut into thin slices
1 tablespoon butter if needed

Heat a frying pan and cook the bacon over a moderately high heat until golden brown and slightly crisp. Lift out, drain on paper towelling and keep warm.

Mix the flour and salt and pepper together and very lightly coat the sliced liver. Brown the liver quickly in the bacon fat, using the butter if necessary and allowing 3 minutes per side for medium rare. Serve the liver topped with bacon.

APPLE SNOW

Australia's own Granny Smith apples are so right and appropriate as the main ingredient in this lovely light summer dessert.

Serves 6

6 Granny Smith cooking apples, peeled, cored and quartered
2 cloves
small piece of lemon rind
1/4 cup water
2 egg whites
1/2 cup sugar

Place the apples, cloves, lemon rind and water in a small saucepan. Cover with lid and cook slowly until the apples are tender. Drain away water and lift out and discard the cloves and lemon peel. Cool and break up with a fork. Beat the egg whites until stiff and gradually beat in the sugar and the cooled apple pulp. Spoon into a serving dish and chill.

SPLIT PEA SOUP

Penny conscious Australian women soaked the split peas to cut down on cooking time and fuel costs. They even saved the rinds of the breakfast bacon before cooking it, but most women felt that a few bacon bones gave a much better flavour and if the soup was cooked for longer there was no need to soak the peas.

Serves 6 - 8

1 1/2 cups split peas
2 medium onions, finely chopped
2 medium carrots, finely chopped
2 celery stalks, finely chopped
6 cups of water
salt to taste
1 teaspoon black peppercorns
1/2 teaspoon dried thyme
2 bay leaves
4 sprig mint, finely chopped
250g (8oz) bacon bones

Place all the ingredients in a large saucepan and bring to the boil. Skim off any scum that rises to the surface. Cover with a lid and cook over a low heat for 3 to 4 hours, stirring every now and then. Add more water if necessary. Serve with croutons.

Croutons

Equal quantities of butter and oil for shallow frying, 2 slices stale bread, cut into 1cm (1/2 inch) cubes. Heat the butter in a small frying pan and cook bread cubes for a few seconds until brown. Drain on kitchen paper.

LAMINGTONS

Lamingtons come in all shapes and sizes from the gigantic handful for the hungry school child to the dainty mouthful for a ladies' afternoon tea party. These squares of butter cake coated with chocolate icing and rolled in a coconut were first made in Queensland in the 1890s and named after Lady Lamington, the wife of the State Governor.

Makes 20

1 butter cake baked in a 18 X 28cm (7 X 12 inch) pan the day before
3 tablespoons boiling water
30g. (1oz) butter
2 level tablespoons cocoa
2 cups icing sugar, sifted
2 cups desiccated coconut (flaked)

Chill the cake for 30 minutes to make it easier to cut. Cut into 5cm (2 inch) squares. Pour the boiling water over the butter in a bowl and blend in the cocoa. Beat in the icing sugar. Using a long pronged fork, dip each square of cake into the chocolate icing and then roll in the coconut. Leave to set on a wire rack. If the icing becomes too thick add a very small amount of hot water. Lamingtons can also be split in halves and filled with whipped cream.

SWEET CURRY

These days gourmet Australian cooks grind their own spices for curries and never ever buy packaged supermarket curry powders. But their mothers and grandmothers used leftover meats to make this surprisingly tasty curry.

Serves 4

2 tablespoons butter
1 large apple, peeled, cored and diced
1 large onion, finely chopped
2 to 4 teaspoons curry powder
500g cooked lean meat, cut into cubes
1 tablespoon fruit chutney
1 tablespoon plum jam
1 banana, peeled and sliced
1 tablespoon sultanas (golden raisins)
2 tablespoons desiccated (flaked) coconut
1 tablespoon lemon juice
salt to taste

Heat the butter in a saucepan and slowly cook the apples, onions and curry powder for 10 minutes, stirring every now and then. Add the meat, chutney, jam, banana, sultanas and coconut. Cover with a lid and cook very slowly for 30 minutes. Season with lemon juice and salt and serve with boiled rice.

PUFTALOONS

These are rather indigestible, fatty and very filling and are only made by sentimental older Australians who remember their mothers cooking them on cold winter's nights. They were always eaten with that extremely sweet distinctively Australian delicacy, golden syrup.

Serves 4

1 cup plain (all purpose) flour
1 level teaspoon baking powder
pinch of salt
1 level teaspoon butter
1/2 cup milk
fat or oil for deep frying

Sift the flour, baking powder and salt together. Rub in the butter with the fingertips and add the milk all at once to make a soft dough. Heat the oil and drop in spoonfuls of the dough. Cook until the underside is golden, turn over and cook the other side. Drain on paper towels and serve immediately with golden syrup (light treacle), honey or jam.

STRAWBERRY SPONGE SANDWICH

Afternoon tea parties were once very popular in Australia and ladies would dress in their best with hats and gloves and drink tea and eat buttered scones, small fish paste and lettuce sandwiches, fancy home made busicuits and light-as -a-feather sponge cakes like this one.

Serves 6

1 1/2 cups plain (all purpose) flour
1 level teaspoon baking powder
pinch of salt
4 eggs whites
1 cup castor (superfine) sugar
4 egg yolks
1 teaspoon melted butter
1/2 cup boiling water

For Decoration
1 cup thickened (heavy) cream
whipped with 1 tablespoon sugar
250g (8oz) strawberries, hulled and halved

Preheat the oven to moderate. Grease two 20cm (8 inch) round pans with butter and dust lightly with a little flour. Sift the flour, baking powder and salt.

Beat the egg whites until stiff but do not dry and gradually beat in the sugar. Beat in the egg yolks one at a time. Very gently fold in the sifted flour, melted butter and boiling water. Divide the mixture evenly between the two prepared tins. Bake in the preheated oven for 20 to 25 minutes or until the cake is firm to the touch and has shrunk a little from the sides. Leave in the pan for two minutes before turning onto a wire rack to cool. When completely cold, place one cake on a serving dish and spread with thickly whipped cream. Place the second sponge on top and decorate with the strawberries.

PAVLOVA

There is always disagreement about who created this wonderful dessert with various Australians claiming the honour. However, the nicest and true story is that it was created in 1935 in Western Australia by a former shearer's cook Herbert Sachse who named it after Russian ballerina Anne Pavlova as he felt it was as light and "airy fairy" as she was when she danced.

Serves 8 to 10

4 egg whites
1 cup castor (superfine) sugar
4 level teaspoons cornflour
1 teaspoon vinegar
1/2 teaspoon vanilla essence
1 cup thickened (heavy) cream, whipped
4 bananas, peeled and sliced
3 passionfruit, halved and seeded
250g (8oz) strawberries, hulled

Preheat oven to hot. Place a sheet of baking parchment on a lightly greased flat baking tray and draw a 18cm (7 inch) circle in the centre. Lightly grease the parchment and dust with a little cornflour.

Beat the egg whites until stiff and gradually beat in the sugar a tablespoon at a time. Beat until the mixture is thick and shiny and the sugar is dissolved. Very gently fold in the cornflour, vinegar and vanilla essence. Spoon into the drawn circle on the baking tray and smooth the top. Reduce the oven heat to slow and place in oven. Cook for 1 1/2 hours. Let stand for 5 minutes before turning onto a serving plate. Remove baking parchment and allow to cool completely before decorating with the whipped cream and fruit.

CHRISTMAS PLUM PUDDING

At Christmas time, most Australians still follow the British traditions of feasting and overeating that are more suited to a very cold December day in England than what can be the hottest day of the year in Australia. Many women try to give their families more sensible cold food and salads but the general feeling is, it doesn't feel like Christmas without the hot roast turkey, duck or pork, the slices of cold ham, the roast potatoes, pumpkin and sweet potato, the two kinds of green vegetable, the brown gravy, the chocolates and the nuts on the table, and of course, the rich, rich Christmas pudding, that everyone still calls a Plum Pudding, even though there are never any plums in it.

Serves 8 to 10
500g (1lb) sultanas (golden raisins)
500g (1lb) currants
250g (8 oz) raisins,chopped
125g (4 oz) mixed peel (candied orange and lemon peel)
125 (4 oz) blanched almonds, chopped
1 to 11/2 cups brandy
500g (1lb) butter
500g (1lb) light brown sugar
8 eggs
250g (8 oz) plain (all purpose) flour
pinch of salt
1 level teaspoon bicarbonate of soda (baking soda)|
1/2 level teaspoon cinnamon
1/2 level teaspoon nutmeg
1/2 level teaspoon ground cloves
1/4 level teaspoon ground ginger
250g (8 oz) fresh white breadcrumbs
1 teaspoon grated lemon rind
1 teaspoon grated orange rind
1/2 teaspoon vanilla essence
2 tablespoons orange marmalade
1 tablespoon treacle

Combine all the fruits and almonds in a bowl and sprinkle on the brandy. Leave to stand for 24 hours. Beat the butter and sugar until light and fluffy and add the eggs one at a time, beating well after each one is added. Sift the flour with all the dry ingredients and mix into the fruit with all the remaining ingredients to make a mixture of dropping consistency. Let stand for 30 minutes. Add extra brandy or fruit juice if the mixture is too dry.

*Cooking variations
continued next page*

CHRISTMAS PLUM PUDDING
Cooking Variations
To cook in a pudding basin.

Grease two 8 cup pudding basins with butter and line the bases with rounds of baking parchment. Spoon the pudding mixture into the bowls to within 4cm (1 1/2 in) of the top, and top with rounds of baking parchment. Cover the basins with two layers of aluminium foil and tie securely with string, adding a loop of string for easier handling. Lower the basins into a large saucepan of rapidly boiling water with the water coming halfway up the sides. Cover a lid and cook with the water continually simmering for 4 hours. Add extra boiling water as needed and do not allow the puddings to cool in the saucepan when cooked. On serving day cook for a further hour.

To cook in a pudding cloth.

Immerse a large square of new but washed unbleached calico in a saucepan of boiling water. Lift out with tongs and spread out flat. Dust lightly with flour. Place the cloth in a large basin and spoon in the pudding mixture. Gather the cloth around the pudding leaving a small space at the top for the pudding to swell. Tie up very tightly with string, adding a loop of string for easier handling. Dust lightly with flour and lower into a large saucepan of boiling water. Cover with a lid and cook with the water continually simmering for 6 hours, adding additional boiling water if needed. Lift out and hang up to dry. On serving day, cook for another 3 hours.

Cooked puddings keep very well and are often made up to twelve months in advance so that the flavours develop and mature.

Brandy Butter
250g (8oz) unsalted butter
1 1/2 cups icing (confectioner's) sugar
4 tablespoons brandy.

Beat the butter and icing sugar until light and fluffy and gradually beat in the brandy. Chill until firm.

BOILED FRUIT CAKE

Many women find that Christmas is upon them long before they expected it and they just don't have the time or they just don't want to make a rich expensive fruit cake and it's then they make this much simpler Boiled Fruit Cake.

2 cups plain (all purpose) flour
2 level teaspoons baking powder
1/2 cup butter
1 cup cold tea or water
1 cup light brown sugar
1 1/2 cups sultanas (golden raisins)
1 1/2 cups currants
1/2 cup glace (candied) cherries
1 level teaspoon cinnamon
1/2 level teaspoon nutmeg
1/2 level teaspoon ground ginger
1/4 level teaground cloves
1 level teaspoon bicarbonate of soda (baking soda)
2 large eggs, lightly beaten

Line a 23cm (9 inch) square cake pan with 2 layers of baking parchment. Sift the flour and baking powder together. Place the butter, tea, brown sugar, dried fruit and spices in a saucepan and bring to the boil. Cook over a low heat for 5 minutes, stirring every now and then. Mix in the bicarbonate of soda and allow to cool completely. Stir in the beaten eggs and sifted flour and baking powder. Spoon into prepared pan and bake in a moderately slow oven for 1 1/4 hours or until a skewer inserted in the centre of the cake comes out dry. If the cake is browning too much, cover loosely with aluminium foil. Leave the cake in the pan to cool.